Minute Manna
and More

Poems by
Fr. Stephen Kluge, O.F.M.

Grateful Leper Publishing
www.grateful-leper.com
Diogenes Ruiz
ISBN: 978-0-9763126-8-0

alannah;
you are a "Saint of God!"
Fr. Steve, fm

DEDICATION

To the many people I call family

CONTENTS

FOREWORD

To the reader,

Thank you for buying this book and I hope you find the poems entertaining. You might find the title misleading "Minute Manna and More" since all the poems are short. I can almost hear some of you asking, "So where's the more?" Actually, you are invited to supply the more. Since there is plenty of room on a page I encourage you to do a line drawing, color a picture, or write a poem of your own in response.

We can all be poets,

      And artists,

      And more,

      It's just that most of us don't know it.

Fr. Stevek, ofm

I wonder what the minnows make
Of those skating
On the ice at the top of the lake.

Sometimes
Silence
Or a whispered
Sigh
Speaks more honestly to God than a
Thesaurus filled tongue.

If death is truly the end,
Then
Even beatified being is
Nothing but
Hellish torment.

MY JUSTIFICATION FOR KILLING A
BEAUTIFUL BLACK BUTTERFLY
I thought
It was
A moth.

Back in the day,
Our lawn was nothing but dandelions,
And we never knew
We could have made a salad
Or better yet,
Wine.

Rosa Parks
Was looking for more than a seat,
She was seeking a merciful heart.
Finding none,
She sat where she could.

Caterpillar sleeps
In a bed of silken sheets
Awakens butterfly.

Awakening too early
 It seems too dark.
But as the sky is illumined
I see a mountain
Blocking the sun.

Grace overwhelms,
Yet we do not drown.
We soar!

Excuses for my own faults
Fall so easily off my tongue.
While words of forgiveness
Sit like a lump in my throat.

Dreams
Leave feelings to be considered.
Or if you will
Grist for reflection's mill.

God is the hostess of the ball:
A wall-flower
Patiently waiting
For Her invitation
To dance.

Ignore the sun at your own peril.
The moon
Waxes and wanes unnoticed by most,
 Reflects
A gentle light
In the darkness of the still
And holy night.

While praying,
Despite the noise within,
I heard the flutter of
Cardinal's wings.

The heart is
An open door
Through which the still
Grace world
Wounded by sin,
Unbidden enters
And is received with a curious
If unequal mix
Of hostility and hospitality.

Cypress trees stand
Stoic silent sentinels
Surveying
Slumbering vacant shells of saints
Waiting in garden tombs.

Apple blossom
Hangs suspended
Mid-air
In a sliver of
Spider's silver silk.

Second guessing yesterday
Is a thief that robs one of the joy of today,
And a roaring beast
That makes one fearful of tomorrow.

A conclave of cardinals
Gathered on
Snow vested ground
Eat
Fallen holly berries
While the world around them
Makes not a sound.

Credit goes to the farmer
For planting the seed.
Words chosen
Enter the unknowable soil of
Heart and mind.
We are all farmers
And must take at least some credit or blame
No matter the harvest.

Is it the tree that grasps
The last of the leaves
Or
The leaf that clings
As the wintry winds blow?

JOHN 8: 1-11
Your stooping to write in the dirt
Says to me
My sins are written in sand.
Why then do I
With sins committed against me
Carve them in stone?

Each morning Lord,
You gift me with grace
 to be
Reborn at breakfast:
Another Easter dawning.
And I feast on the question,
"Who would you have me be today?"

I am not grateful for
Crumbs and morsels
While I covet the
Whole loaf.

Why is it that
What we don't understand
We fear;
What we fear
We learn to hate;
What we hate
We must eradicate?

When I pray
The rosary
My most honest prayer happens in the
Space
Between the beads.

Today I prayed,
"Meet me half way, O Lord."
Then God replied,
"How can I meet you half way
When I am always already with you?"

If only insight
Was as quickly lit as
Wit.

I spent a great deal of time today
Counting my blessings:
Four hundred ninety-nine to be exact.
Oh,
I forgot one.

Like dandelions,
Prayers pop into my mind
And I impatiently wait
For their roots to reach down
Into my heart and hands and feet.

Something is amiss
In America's pursuit of life, liberty, and happiness
We kill our children.

The recipe for human nature
Is so delicious that the
Divine chef
Just knew
She had to have a taste.

Come away with me.
Whisper your dreams and sorrows.
I will hide them,
Heal them,
Keep them safe,
Until the bright tomorrow.

There is nothing
More beautiful
Than an
Opened church door.

In the early hours of the morning,
Amid the false privacy of some low hanging branches,
I spied two robins mating.
The female seemed ambivalent
Or unaware of
All the attention being paid her.

Sometimes I am a tiny grand of sand,
An irritant
On the tender heart of God
Waiting for grace
To change me into a pearl.

*The next three poems were written at San Damiano Retreat
Center in Danville, CA*

Leaves,
Like ladles holding
Dew and rain,
Become bathtubs for beetles,
And other creeping crawling things.

My sacred silence was interrupted
By the hum
Hum
Hum
Of a hummingbird's wings.

Still not ready to appear
In all her naked glory,
An iris remained
Clothed in her bud.

Foolishly
I have feasted on
 Bitter grapes and
Sour wine.
Though
Patient prayer
Transforms their taste
To rich merlot and
Raisin cakes.

They are named Iron and Dark,
Renaissance,
Enlightenment,
Modernity including
Pre and Post.
But some say our age
Is nameless.
But still we must try.
Since we live under the gloom of
Mushroom cloud,
How about,
The Time of Existential Modernity.

I held a flickering firefly,
But distracted by the darkness,
I didn't notice it fly away.

Though eclipsed by a
Tiny moon,
The enormous sun
Still shines.

Before sunrise
Birds
Chirp lauds
Greeting each other and the Lord
And only then
Go out and search for morning manna.

A withered oak leaf
Caught in spider's web
Makes a safe hammock
For a sleeping beetle.

Surprised,
The humming bird
Hovered and with
Tilted head
Stared into my eyes.
I wonder what she saw within
That made her fly away.

I am too often
Standing knee deep
In the kiddie pool
Thinking
I am swimming.

I wonder,
How wet
Did Jesus get
While walking on the sea?

When leaves have fallen from the trees,
It's then we see
The twigged homes of squirrels and birds.
When my green goes
Then will be revealed
The home that I have built of
Stone, and twigs, and sin, and
Grace.

Grace is wild:
A shimmering personal thing
That transforms the harshest winter
Into eternal spring.

Sin sticks to us
Like pollen
On a bee.
But grace is
A fountain of
Overflowing reverie.

Wrapped in routine,
Each day,
For those with eyes to see,
Is filled with mystery.

I'd rather think it's
Fear,
Not cruelty
That causes us to kill
The spider, the wasp, or the bee
As they go about their tasks of the day.

As the summer season ends,
Nature throws a party
With trees
Letting loose leaves;
Multi-colored confetti
Carpeting the forest floor.

Since birds chirp
In so many ways,
It's sinful to think
There's only one way to pray.

Grace is sticky
And smudges us
Like pollen from a lilly.

Of course the sheep are saved.
You are after all,
The Lamb of God.
So what can we hope
For the goats?

The bird must fall
Before she begins to fly;
To join the flight,
We, to ourselves, must die.

What does it say of the boy
(much less the man)
Who grieves the dog,
More than the dad.

All crowns are grass
Save for one,
That sits atop the head of God's only
begotten son.

On Thanksgiving,
Pity not the turkey,
For at the end of the day,
It is we who are stuffed.

Whether I have sown
More wheat or tares
Only time will tell
For all that I have ever done
Will be revealed by candle, book, and bell.

Seeking a home
Wisdom finds temporary shelter
And when ignored
Becomes like a bubble on the wind.

During the third rainy day
I began to realize how
Fierce and unrelenting is
God's love for me.

My mourning heart needs silence
So I might hear
My blessings sing.

Whether full
Or crescent,
I am moon
Reflecting the light of the sun.

Christ is Risen,
And rising,
And rising,
And rising,
Into our eternally expansive God.

Fully clothed for the scorching heat of summer,
Naked during winter's chill,
To me,
Trees are a mystery.

The light of Christ,
Not the dark of my sin,
Compels me to go forward.

Perhaps in prayer
One should seek not answers,
But better questions.

I did not have to be,
And yet,
I am
For God desired to be known through me.

My Sister Moon
Has no light of her own,
Yet shines
Due to the generosity of
Our Brother Sun.

An eternal rose
Loses its' beauty
Not in itself
But in the beholders eye.

Kindness requires a seeing eye
An open heart,
An ear that hears the cry
And hands that reach out to help.

Satan smiles
Not snarls
Behind a human mask,
Licks his lips and whispers,
"Believe me,
I'm on your side."

We each drew hearts
In the sand
Where the waves meet the shore,
And we each had to choose
To draw them again,
And again,
And again.

The well will run dry,
And when it does,
Let your tears mingle
In the still moist mud.

In the desert of prayer
I find myself not deserted
For there too Christ does dwell.
My fast become a sweet dessert
As I give as alms my arms
And hands
And heart as well
To fill another's unknown need
And then the desert of my prayer
With flowers blooms and swells.

Now I know it,
I am not called to be a poet.

ACKNOWLEDGMENTS

A Word of Thanks...

To God... Who sustains my life.

To my family who have been the hook that begins many homilies...Yes, you are holy.

To my brother friars...For accepting me...Twice.

To the Poor Clares in Chesterfield, N.J....You are always home when I visit.

To the Saints of God on Long Beach Island, N.J....Through you Christ called me.

To the Saints of God in St. Francis Parish, Raleigh, N.C...Through you Christ healed me.

ABOUT THE AUTHOR

Fr. Stephen K., OFM is a Franciscan parish priest.

"The antidote to fear is Faith
And the fruit of faith is Charity"

Fr. Stephen K

Made in the USA
Columbia, SC
11 August 2023

21418396R00050